Individually both Zen and Permaculture have a powerful

potential to inspire c

perspective on the w   in

it. Stefan Geyer has,

combined these with   ned

through experience, giving insight into the natural world

and, ultimately, our own nature.

Mark Boyle, author of Moneyless Manifesto *and* Drinking
Molotov Cocktails With Gandhi

Here is a beautiful, visionary and spacious dance between
Zen and permaculture. We are invited to explore the
magic, hope and possibilities that permaculture contains
for each individual, humanity and the planet. The vision is
grounded with useful tips that we can bring into our lives
to have immediate positive impact.

Looby Macnamara, author of People and Permaculture *and*
7 Ways to Think Differently

Inspiring thoughts that helped me to focus when lost in design.

Petra Krubeck, Permakultur Institut, Germany

A fresh and fascinating look at a life changing subject.
Really enjoyable.

Aranya, author of Permaculture Design – Step By Step

Permaculture is a philosophical approach which trains us to reframe situations to find regenerative solutions. This book uses an older thought provoking approach to deepen the conversation about how permaculture can be applied.
Suzi High, former International Co-ordinator for the Permaculture Association, teacher and nurse

Even the most experienced designer can sometimes get caught up in over-thinking and 'analysis paralysis'. Stefan's Zenarchist approach is a timely reminder that permaculture design is about keeping it light, keeping it simple, and just flipping doing it...
Graham Burnett, author of Permaculture – A Beginner's Guide *and* The Vegan Book of Permaculture

It is small in size but infinite in wisdom. Without ever being dogmatic Stefan conveys the essence of what is permaculture design, as well as the joys and pitfalls found on the journey of becoming a permaculturist delivered, in a meditative, self-reflective, poetic and no-nonsense style. The tenets of Zen engage in meaningful dialogue with the art of permaculture design. *Zen in the Art of Permaculture Design* is a must read for any aspiring, curious or seasoned permaculture designer.
Teresa Pereira, permaculture designer at Grow Gaia

A lovely book that reminds us of the importance of doing nothing, sitting still and just thinking before setting out to create beautiful and genuinely labour-saving Permaculture designs.
Tom Hodgkinson, editor, idler.co.uk

By concerning itself with just those subtle, radical shifts in perspective that (ideally) accompany prolonged exposure to ecological design thinking, Stefan Geyer helps illuminate some of the slipperiest aspects of the permaculture worldview. In doing so, he makes a real and strikingly original contribution to permaculture literature.
Rafter Sass-Ferguson PhD, Agroecologist and teacher

Exploring permaculture through the perspective of Zen Buddhism is a masterstroke. If you expect tips on gardening you will be disappointed, but if you want to know what permaculture is you find a thousand answers here.
Tomas Remiarz, author and permaculture teacher

Zen
in the Art of
Permaculture Design

Stefan Geyer

Design and Illustrations by Fred Deakin
Published by Permanent Publications

Published by
Permanent Publications
Hyden House Ltd
The Sustainability Centre
East Meon, Hampshire GU32 1HR
United Kingdom
Tel: +44 (0)1730 823 311
Fax: +44 (0)1730 823 322
Email: enquiries@permaculture.co.uk
Web: www.permanentpublications.co.uk

Distributed in the USA by
Chelsea Green Publishing Company, PO Box 428,
White River Junction, VT 05001
www.chelseagreen.com

Design and illustrations by Fred Deakin

Printed in the UK by CPI Antony Rowe, Chippenham, Wiltshire

All paper from FSC certified mixed sources

The Forest Stewardship Council (FSC) is a non-profit
international organisation established to promote the
responsible management of the world's forests. Products
carrying the FSC label are independently certified to
assure consumers that they come from forests that are
managed to meet the social, economic and ecological
needs of present and future generations.

British Library Cataloguing-in-Publication Data
A catalogue record for this book is available from the British Library

ISBN 978 1 85623 289 0

I'd like to

Offer something

To help you

But in the Zen school

We don't have a single thing!

Ikkyu

Foreword

You may know a bit about Zen already.

Or about Permaculture.

Perhaps both.

But if you don't, you're lucky – what a treat you have in store!
In this beautiful book, Stefan Geyer weaves together these
two liberating systems of thought – ancient and modern,
inward- and outward-facing – and gives practical tips on
how you can apply them to your own world. Stefan is a
man who lives by these insights, and shares them freely,
and you could not hope to find a better guide.

John-Paul Flintoff

author of How To Change The World

Introduction:
A view from
the mountain

In which we set the scene and begin on our journey...

Permaculture is revolution disguised as organic gardening.
Mike Feingold

For Zen students a weed, which for most people is
worthless, is a treasure. With this attitude, whatever you do,
life becomes an Art.
Shunryu Suzuki

Permaculture is to ecology what engineering is to physics –
the application of fundamental patterns and principles to
solve real-life challenges.
Tomas Remiarz

Why read this book?

This book is an attempt to show how Permaculture,
infused with insights from the Zen tradition, can be a modern
method of great liberation from our society's present
woes. It aims to empower and embolden those that wish to
creatively engage with the wickedly complex problems of
today, while not adding to the chaos and mess – helping us
to consciously act in our environment with grace and clarity.
It is for those who want to live on a healthy thriving planet,
in a fair society where people care for each other, want
this for their children and grandchildren too, and are
interested in figuring out how to do it for themselves.

If you're looking for a book on gardening, this isn't it.
Neither is this a 'How to' manual. If fact it will quite likely
leave you with more questions than you began with.

For practical techniques, step by step instructions or 101 ideas there are dozens of clear, well researched, Permaculture titles out there, written by experts in their fields, with knowledge born of patient, hard-won experience. Seek them out in the appendices at the end of the book when you need help in tackling new projects.

In this exploration into some of the deeper themes in the Permaculture landscape, we try to get to the heart of the matter – how on earth are we to know what to do, to judge our actions, to begin what needs to be done, to continue when all seems lost, and to adapt to whatever comes next? Permaculture Design is the earth repair toolbox for the 21st Century; how are you going to use it?

Permaculture: meeting human needs while preserving and increasing ecosystem health.

Rafter Sass-Ferguson

Why Permaculture?

Permaculture = a new regenerative culture.

Permaculture Design = the method to get there.

People often come to Permaculture because they are stuck. They see their precious world is in a mess, and want to help. Having maybe tried their luck with whatever the mainstream has to offer, they have become disenchanted and are looking for something new, are looking for answers. Luckily for us all, Permaculture is brimming over not just with answers, but with solutions.

Often erroneously thought of as an organic gardening technique, Permaculture is more accurately viewed as a worldwide collaborative effort to redesign our impact on the planet. This includes a sort of global open-source (wiki style) project that we're all adding to year after year – building up a giant database of everything we're ever going to need to help us vision and design a truly healthy, thriving future.

Permaculture is a multifaceted diamond, meaning many things to many people. It can also be a puzzling creature. Yet in trying to catch this elusive beast, care has been taken in this book not to tame its nature. With this in mind we'll dive into a waterfall of possible questions, asking: What are the characteristics of Permaculture? Where does Permaculture thinking naturally take us? What spirit underpins it all? Where do we want to get to?

You don't do Permaculture, you use it in what you do.
Larry Santoyo

Permaculture is not the last word, a magic bullet or panacea – but is more like a pinch of salt that enhances every other flavour. Although it is helpful to designers, architects and planners, Permaculture can in no way replace the years of hard graft demanded to learn a subject, skill or trade – it just brings an extra something, a shift in perception that changes everything.

The intention here is to articulate that shift – to show how Permaculture can not only be a design methodology, a multidisciplinary catalyst, or a set of clever slogans or heuristics, but also a worldview, and within all of this, a process of awakening. Permaculture asks us to wake up and become conscious of our environment and, further, to become conscious of ourselves in our environment. As we become intimately aware of how nature works, we become more sensitive to our place within the natural world, and in doing so see into our own nature – inexorably bound together as one with our environment. This knowledge, and experiencing this first hand, can be transcendental.

Seek not the path of the ancients,
Seek that which the ancients sought!
Basho

Why Zen?

Zen is a unique way of being, often seeing itself as separate from the religion of Buddhism – a direct and pragmatic way of being in the world, whose 1,500 years of history has much to inform the young discipline of Permaculture. Although Zen is fundamentally beyond the comprehension of the rational mind, and Permaculture is a child of scientific thought, they need not be uncomfortable bed-fellows. As we will see, Zen can fertilise Permaculture thinking very naturally, yielding unexpected yet tasty fruits.

Zen is not the focus of this book or explicitly mentioned in the text, yet it is in the feel of it. The book is flavoured with, steeped in, and coloured throughout with helpful references and quotes, nudging attitudes and powerful insights taken from Zen Buddhism. Rather than comparing concepts taken from Zen and Permaculture, for example the Zen Precepts with the Permaculture Ethics, it is understood that both are part of a greater whole. The path offered here is one towards being present to where we are, what 'right action' in the Buddhist sense might actually look like today, and how we can enquire into it.

Permaculture is a direction not a destination.

Graham Bell

The layout.

This little book of quiet lightning and gentle earthquakes is written as a thought-provoking journey of enquiry and discovery, with the narrative arc loosely following a simple yet classic Permaculture Design process – SADI (Survey, Analysis, Design, Implementation). After the opening chapter, which explores the question "What actually is Permaculture?" we start with our Survey – an observation of the natural world and where we find ourselves.

We then move to Analysis – how the myriad of information gathered in the Survey can be understood, and finally what to do with it all – Design a plan. The final chapter weaves around thoughts on Implementation – how to follow through on actually getting things done in the world, without which all this design stuff is just hot air.

Each page illustrates a Permaculture idea or theme that fits within the arc, but which also works well read on its own. They are purposefully designed not to be the last word on a subject, but as a beginning, to act as a catalyst for new thought, your own. The text is unapologetically short, and asks the reader to play with what's being presented. Hold the words in meditation for a while, see how the ideas can be incorporated into your own way of doing, and look for what is missing or can be elaborated on.

Onwards.

Pop this book in your pocket and dip in when you're feeling stuck. Use Permaculture Design as a gateway and catalyst. Instead of being crushed by the heavy weight of the industrial destructoculture that tangles us in its seemingly inescapable net, Permaculture offers us emancipation from old worn out models of the world, and emboldens us to think in joyfully expansive, daringly experimental and creatively caring new ways.

In walking, just walk.

In sitting, just sit.

Above all, don't wobble.

Yün-men

Chapter One:
The uncarved block

In which we tackle the question: what exactly is Permaculture?

There is nothing in a caterpillar that tells you it's going to be a butterfly.

R. Buckminster Fuller

All models are wrong, but some are useful.

George Box

To be independent in the true sense, we have to forget everything which we have in our mind and discover something quite new and different moment after moment. When you study you should have a general house cleaning of your mind. Take everything out and clean it thoroughly. You may bring everything back in again – do so one by one, but only if it is necessary otherwise your mind will become crowded with old, useless junk.
S. Suzuki

Drop what you think you know.

If you really want to understand Permaculture, it is necessary to ditch all your preconceived ideas and become an independent thinker – independent, yet connected to the whole. Give up the idea of 'sustainability' or 'environment', and what they have come to mean to you, as their baggage is heavy for the journey ahead – and these tired concepts will only hold you back from seeing what is really happening in the world, and therefore what needs to be done. Wipe the slate clean – which is, of course, an impossible ask, but do it anyway. Be prepared to slay some sacred cows, lose any hollow traditions and demand proof when it may be uncomfortable to do so. The short history of Permaculture is gladly littered with colourful folk that have done just that – arrogant pioneers, stubborn heretics, tedious pedants and righteous rebels. Permaculture is the language, among others, of the rebel farmer, the community builder, the armchair activist, the tough-loving parent and the social entrepreneur. So you'll be in good company when you speak out or act in ways that may at times be considered outrageous in polite society. Stick your neck out, get your head cut off, grow another head, do it again.

We're simply an ecosystem living within a larger ecosystem. And whatever we do has consequences.
Aranya

Everything's connected to everything.

Permaculture started out in the 1970s in Australia as an integrated systems approach to living sustainably, based around growing perennial food crops – that is, crops that do not need to be replanted annually, but continue to grow year after year. The underlying reason perennial food crops were chosen over annuals, was in response to the question 'How do we live with the least effort for the optimum effect?' That is still the same difficult question asked of us today. The answers are to be found all around in nature's incredible abundance and diversity – for example mimicking a native forest to create a forest garden, which, among other things, produces a variety of food and fuel. Permaculture started with food because it's so central to our lives, connected to every aspect of how our society is built. Yet when we stop to consider how we might start to grow healthy food, sooner or later we will notice that we can't have good soil without clean water, and we can't have clean water with air pollution, and we can't have healthy air while endlessly burning fossil fuels, which we somehow need to burn to drive to work (that we might not even enjoy) to pay for the food we need in the first place! So if we grow even a little of our own food, with one stroke we're beginning to disentangle ourselves from the uncaring, complex industrial culture many people feel trapped inside today – making gardening a political act. Understanding this, that it's virtually impossible to separate food from every other part of our existence, over the years, through sheer necessity and viral creativity, Permaculture has evolved into something much broader than just dealing with agriculture – it now embraces all aspects of how we live and are to build a future that will last for generations.

A monk asked Tozan, "What is the Buddha?"
Tozan answered, "Three pounds of flax!"
Mumon

What is it you need?

Is Permaculture an attitude, a method, an approach,
a philosophy, a direction, a destination, a vision, or
all of these? Maybe it's better not to ask "What is
Permaculture?" but to ask instead what you need to solve
all those seemingly unsolvable questions that arise from
this complicated ethical puzzle that is modern life – and
make that your Permaculture. How can we be part of the
world and not be caught up, lost, or frozen and unable
to act? Find out what you need, and design how you're
going to make it happen. If a definition of Permaculture
is not big enough for you, widen it. It's yours to do with
what you will. Expanding the boundaries of possibility
allows you to engage with the many-headed fire-
breathing beast of the current globalised world. Your
Permaculture can be unique, and free to evolve, mutate
and surprise – and be 100% relevant, changing moment
to moment, allowing you space to dive deeper and

deeper into what's possible. A good practice to sharpen the mind is to regularly write down on a piece of paper your latest definition of Permaculture. This way you can roll it up and throw it on the compost heap – better still, use it as mulch. It might seem as if the definition is so broad, that it would encompass anything and everything, but it doesn't. For although Permaculture is an empty vessel – an umbrella term that is ready, willing and capable of covering an infinite variety of ideas – to hold diverse tools, principles, techniques, models, strategies, goals and a myriad other things that can help us envisage and design a new world culture in harmony with the Earth, it has at its heart a set of powerfully simple Ethics, which act as a keen filter, and a personal benchmark to judge your actions in the world. So simply look around and feel free to take whatever ideas you need from wherever possible to help you achieve your aims, making sure they also serve the greater good. Without which, it just wouldn't be Permaculture.

If we are mindful of each thing we do, even if we do the exact same things as others, we can enter directly into the world of Zen.
Thich Nhat Hanh

Where are you headed?

Reminding us to be ever mindful, the three Ethics of Earthcare, Peoplecare and Fair Share are the responsive beating heart of Permaculture – the North Star to which it is helpful to set our compass. What do these terms mean to you? Consider them individually, for example, when contemplating Earthcare, what would you include or leave out? What does the idea of caring invoke in you? Then think about the three together – how do they interact and overlap? Do they cover everything? What might be missing? These simple yet broad ideas can be taken on many levels – working as a set of values or morals, a declaration of intentions or aspirations, boundaries to keep us in check, guarding against mission drift or impulsive actions, and they can also be used as a measure of the quality in our work. As life is often messy, difficult and painfully random, let the Ethics give you strength to continue in your chosen direction. Acting as a thread that helps guide us through the moral maze of living in the modern world, where compromises will always need to be made, they help us know what to do next – which choice to make, where to put our energy, when to withdraw it or even use it to block. The Permaculture Ethics aren't rocks in the ground, but starting points for enquiry. They ask us to open out our thinking, continually question and pay attention – urging us to stay awake, and choose our own path rather than blindly follow. The Permaculture Ethics are not external laws designed to make you feel guilty if you don't obey them, pressurising you to fit a particular mould, but are more of a supportive internal map and, importantly, they are for Us – it's up to each one of us to set our own parameters. Make them your own, asking at each step – does this action fit with my Ethics, and if so, how well?

My real dwelling
Has no pillars
And no roof either
So the rain cannot soak it
And the wind cannot blow it down.
Ikkyu

The only limit is the imagination of the designer.
Bill Mollison

Why?

When starting out in any Permaculture project, always
ask yourself the great Why? – Why bother? What
difference would it make? This will greatly impact the
goals, the purpose or function of the project at hand.
Why? will be the essence of the vision, the strategy, the
mission. Where do you want it to go? Why? This is the
nub of the client interview (which is also very useful to
do on yourself), and is the place to regularly return to,
however uncomfortable or disruptive it may be, as ideas,
reasons and orientations change. Spend a while on
Why? until it's well-articulated. Are you sure it's going to
make the world a better place, and won't simply add
more chaos? Is it definitely worth the energy? Ask Why?
like a little child, following the answer again with yet
another Why? Get to the heart of it, and when you do,
paint it on a big board, write it on the back of your
hand, and tattoo it backwards on your forehead. The
answer to Why? will dictate everything that comes after,

yet often we don't realise what whole-system goal we're serving, for as odd as it may sound, this crucial point is often overlooked or never thought through. This may be the reason many people intuitively can't trust multinational corporations, which spend so much time and energy covering up their real Why? with happy colours and smiling faces, because no matter how much corporate social responsibility they muster, it's clear that their whole structure is designed primarily for profit. If we get this one thing wrong, all our subsequent efforts will be misdirected. With this vital information, we can unhook our important fundamental needs from the perhaps narrow strategies we may have already decided upon, helping us broaden our horizons. There may be many ways to skin our particular cat. What basic needs are asking to be met? Don't move forward until you know this.

We have more possibilities available in each
moment than we realize.
Thich Nhat Hanh

How?

Your boat in the swirling sea of information and
decisions is your chosen Design Framework – take your
pick from the many out there; it doesn't matter which
you choose. It is useful, and some would almost say
essential, to give your work form. The framework structure
is there to help you in times of obclarity and for when
you wander off topic for too long – but remember not
to imprison yourself in a cage of your own design.
Your boat to get you across the water is useless to you
once you've reached the other side. The framework
supports you like the safe arms of a friend, giving you
the freedom to boldly dream, extravagantly brainstorm,
and dare to invent without getting lost in your fantasies,
bringing you back down to reality to harvest and sort
your ideas, and offering you the space and licence to
do it again and again. Once you have discovered the
underlying need you wish to be met, pause as long as

you can bear it; this pause will give you ample space for your judgement-free observation, yielding information to then coolly analyse, from which you can construct your intelligent design – ready to implement and act out in the world. Once you've actually manifested your design, whatever type of project it might be, you can then once more observe – How did it go? What went well? What could have been better? With these new observations to analyse, the next iteration of your design cycle has already begun. Take small steps, but take each one like a giant leap. That is, unbundle your thoughts and actions, wait and think things through so you know you are not reacting blindly through habit or emotion. In this way you can make sure that whatever you do will be for the good of the whole, in tune with Permaculture's Ethics, and you'll not need to resort to anything that puts your environment out of balance.

If you meet the Buddha on the road, kill him.
Linji

Light your own lamp.

Permaculture is not only wary of authority – it consciously,
jovially, and regularly discriminates against it, promoting
autonomy at every corner. The freedom of autonomy and
self-determination keeps life fresh, dynamic and bountiful.
Only when unrestricted, can we and our projects blossom
new emergent properties in ways unforeseen and
revolutionary. Having the ability to self-organise is the
strongest form of resilience – this is evolution in action.
As our projects evolve in complexity, so we need to
allow them the space and time to demonstrate their own
identity. In this way the practitioner is asked to cultivate a
stance of healthy disregard to anyone claiming to be in
possession of superior knowledge – such as how you
should 'do' Permaculture, or what a 'Permaculture answer'
to a question might be – other than more questions
(or 'it depends'). The one-size-fits-all answer is a trap,
a red-herring and a dead end – and lazily using it will

only end in misery and confusion for all concerned. That doesn't mean there aren't wonderfully instructive teachers out there who could show every one of us a thing or two; it's more that although they can hand you the baton, only you can run with it. This grassroots Do-It-Yourself/Be-Yourself attitude promotes autonomy, and is one of the reasons Permaculture has spread so virally over the last few decades. Part of its attractiveness is that everyone is offered the chance to be part of the living vernacular culture as they are – instead of going to a gallery to see the work of 'the professional artist' paraded as genius, you're invited to create your own art piece together in community, and be part of a dynamic local tapestry that stays fresh by always changing, mutating and reinventing itself.

Harmonizing opposites by going back to their source is
the distinctive quality of the Zen attitude, the Middle Way:
embracing contradictions, making a synthesis
of them, achieving balance.
Taisen Deshimaru

Bring it all to light.

Permaculture is covertly political, publicly apolitical and
genuinely meta-political. Taking the position that the only
ethical decision is to take responsibility for our own
existence and that of our children, Permaculture's aim is
to work out how we can meet as many of our needs
with our own resources as possible. Implicit in this is
the recognition that we exist in a wider society that we
too need to care for and help shape for the better.
Because it's clear we are all intricately bound together,
all affected by what goes on in the world; Permaculture
isn't interested in taking sides but is more concerned with
the good of the whole. The matter at hand gives us no more
time to be childishly divisive, defensively antagonistic or
blindly dogmatic, demanding instead collaboration,
co-production and convergence. Allowing libertarian,

conservative, socialist and anarchist to exist in one person, Permaculture seeks to weave and entwine the various degrees of left and right into a basket that can hold all views, no matter the seeming contradictions, and which can carry the weight of the world's troubles and still have space for being outrageously positive. It does this by simply bringing everything to light – slowing down, getting out of the way, making the world conscious of what's going on, airing it all, naming the obvious and delving down for the not so obvious. This opens up what might seem fixed and finished into a whole new connected landscape, giving everything space in which to move around, evolve and find context. This perspective can witness thesis, antithesis and synthesis unfolding, but always asks – is there yet another way to get all our needs met?

Nan-in, a Japanese master during the Meiji era (1868-1912), received a university professor who came to inquire about Zen. Nan-in served tea. He poured the visitor's cup full, and then kept on pouring. The Professor watched the overflow until he could no longer restrain himself. "It is overfull. No more will go in!" "Like this cup," Nan-in said, "you are full of your own opinions and speculations. How can I show you Zen unless you first empty your cup?"

Paul Reps in Zen Flesh, Zen Bones

Chapter Two: Observing from stillness

In which we study the art of mindful surveying...

Because the world is not going anywhere there is no hurry. One may as well "take it easy" like nature itself. This is a first principle in the study of Zen and of any Far Eastern art: hurry, and all that it involves, is fatal. For there is no goal to be attained. The moment a goal is conceived it becomes impossible to practice the discipline of the art, to master the very rigor of its technique.

Alan Watts

Trying to understand is like straining through muddy water. Have the patience to wait! Be still and allow the mud to settle.

Lao Tzu

If you are unable to find the truth right where you are,
where else do you expect to find it?
Dögen

Start with observation.

Permaculture Design always begins with good observation
– the lengthier, the better. There is no way around this fact,
no easy way out, no skipping this step or doing it with half
your attention. Relax into it. Practise by leaning back and
watching dust floating effortlessly through a sunbeam, or
observe how your body feels differently from one moment
to the next – the more you open yourself uncritically to the
world, the more it'll open itself to you. Let go of yourself in
mindful observation, so that you become that which you
observe. Observe things as they are, not as you want them
to be – this is pivotal to Permaculture Design. Right Observation includes the difficult business of peeling away our
cultural conditioning, our years of factory education and
decades of personal and societal bias. This is no mean feat
– many try, and still layer after onion layer comes off,
seemingly without end. Yet this process slowly wipes the

dirt of prejudice from our eyes and our vision becomes clearer as time goes on. Whatever our project or remit, we need to be sure that before we dive in and influence what is going on with our actions, even in a subtle way, we wait a while and watch how it behaves. Slow right down, and enjoy being unhurried. It doesn't mean our responses can't be a lightning bolt of action and clarity – like the tongue of a quiet yet alert frog, waiting on a lily pad, when it catches a fly passing by. Classic Permaculture thinking states that before we begin anything major on a piece of land, we should observe it for one whole year, watching it change through the seasons – so it is also with every project, whether it involves transport, economics, housing, our community or anything else. Observe the cycles and patterns, and wait. Get to know it intimately, in every pore of your body. Meditate on it and be curious. Where are its edges (what are the boundaries)? What occupies its head (what concepts are floating about)? What are its hands manifesting (what is coming out of it all)? How does its heart beat (what are its rhythms)? Observation always comes before analysis, which comes before design. There can be no doubt, any time spent in observation will reward tenfold.

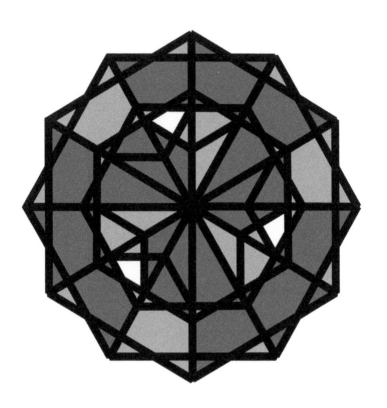

Old pond

Leap, splash!

A frog.

Basho

When we hear the other person's feelings and needs,
we recognize our common humanity.
Marshall Rosenberg

The power of listening.

When making a Survey we need to talk to everyone
involved, the more the merrier – who knows what might
pop up that changes everything, or uncovers an elephant
in the room. So right observation, of course, includes the
essential yet delicate power of listening. If we listen just as
we observe – with an aware, non-judgemental openness,
all manner of information opens out to us, like the petals of
a flower to the morning sun. Although to listen is to receive,
it requires active attention. In conversation, this attention is
needed to notice ourselves itching to jump in – so take a
pause before you answer, otherwise you may end up
projecting your own thoughts onto theirs, or miss an important
piece of information. We need to listen to understand and
connect rather than debate, and be sure to clarify anything
we don't understand, not pulling back from asking direct,
probing, or possibly difficult questions – otherwise we'll be

doing all parties a disservice and wasting everyone's time. Shying away from points begging for our attention and curiosity leads us down the path of bland mediocrity, passive compliance and creative poverty. Ask for clarification until you actually get it, and then say what you've garnered back to them, out loud, acting as a mirror. See what happens – does the person shrink back or do they come alive? Put no emphasis on right and wrong, good and bad, but simply acknowledge things as they are, and reflect this back. Don't find arguments to back up your own opinions about what they are saying, or prompt them into what you consider to be correct – use clean non-guiding language. Find out what touches that person, makes them feel alive. Ask until you get to the real reasons, the core and sometimes hidden, maybe unconscious, needs asking to be met.

Look deep into nature and you will
understand everything better.
Einstein

Nature, the great teacher.

With well over four and a half billion years to work out
many effortless solutions to some very tricky problems,
Nature has much to teach us about how to design with
beautiful efficiency and breath-taking elegance. Careful,
protracted observation of Nature's manifold variations
helps us tap into the huge intelligence out there simply
waiting for us to pay attention to it. This is especially true if
we observe from the perspective of being intrinsically part of
Nature ourselves – that is, we are not in any way separate;
we are Nature looking back at itself. A great way to soak
up this immeasurable wisdom is to patiently immerse
ourselves in the untouched wilderness of virgin forests and
jungles, deserts and tundra, or any sea and landscape that
has been left to its own devices. However, it is not necessary
to travel far and wide in search of this elusive other, the wild
is paradoxically also easily accessible to every urban dweller

– simply get on your hands and knees and enter the microscopic world beneath your feet where the earth is alive with spongey mosses, surprising fungi and dynamic insects, or walk the forgotten, unkempt, unnoticed patches of trees, bushes and weeds along railway lines and at the back of and in between our houses. When designing, let the wild reach in and touch your environment in unexpected ways, and let it into your own life too, allowing it to reveal the surprising untapped richness you hold within. These potent wild spaces, full of life in every niche and scale, are so important for us, often wilderness-starved, civilised folk, that without paying attention to them our learning can at best be only a shadow of its vast potential.

The menu is not the food.
Alan Watts

We make sense of the world through patterns.

As we slow down and start to observe the world more
closely, we may begin to notice regularities and repetitions,
elements appearing and reoccurring in a predictable way
– in Permaculture we put great store in these patterns.
Patterns can unlock the secret code to how Nature works,
understanding how it solves problems, and thereby learning
how to tackle our own difficulties and design issues. Nature
is so full to the brim with patterns it's difficult to know
where to begin – waves, fractals, cracks, ribs, or lobes;
patterns in the landscape – edges, centres, holes or bridges;
patterns in our behaviours – learnt, addictive, eccentric or
passed down. Luckily, our brains are hardwired to find
patterns – it's one way that we understand the world.
When you notice a pattern, whether old or new, try to find
out why it's being used. What is it doing? Why has evolution
chosen this pattern and not another? Some patterns make
a surface area larger, like our deeply convoluted brains,

or smaller like a spikey curled-up hedgehog. Why does the snail shell grow in a spiral? What effect does it have? Where else in the world can we find spirals? How would things be different if another pattern were used? The branching pattern, that can be seen in river deltas and lightning, in our lungs and veins, water pipes and electricity wiring, family trees and group hierarchies, can be seen in two ways – either starting with a single point, able to spread out indefinitely covering as wide an area as possible; or the opposite, bringing a multiplicity of places eventually to one focal point. Where can you use this pattern? Many patterns in the world are not so clear, or take time to reveal themselves, and their meaning. Look for webs, circles, hexagons, cones, zigzags, stars, etc. How can we use the information that patterns give us to understand what is going on, and where they may help us in our designs? When we use patterns like colours on the palette of an artist painting a landscape, we expand our range of choices, combinations and possibilities.

Quantum physics reveals a basic oneness of the universe.
Erwin Schrodinger

Choose your boundaries.

In charting the panorama of patterns long enough we come,
sooner or later, to the realisation that everything is indubitably,
fundamentally connected. In this all-encompassing oneness,
the mind seeks to understand the world by packaging
things into manageable chunks and carves out areas to
work on one at a time. When surveying a new property for
example, where the boundaries are drawn can make a
huge difference to how we perceive the area. We may
remark "This is the garden and this is the house which
backs onto the neighbour's garage", but as a Permaculture
designer we need to forget this persuasive mindplay,
our arbitrary choice of focus, and see it all as one.
Include the whole area, not only the views, the roads,
the winds and the sun, but also the tired owner, the nosy
neighbour and the incontinent dog. In this way we can see
things in their wider, multidimensional context – connected.
Then, whatever we choose to create will have a good

chance of fitting seamlessly into the wider environment. Boundaries are Edges – where two systems meet, often forming a third often more fertile and bountiful place, like when two cultures collide to form something new and creative, such as an innovative music or architectural style. Another form of this is the Chaordic Edge – the dynamic, ever-changing and highly productive tension where chaos and order meet, like relationships within groups or working with animals. Designs, plans and strategies live essentially on this dynamic edge, as they are always full of wishful thinking, approximations of what we hope to control in the future, and are subject to constant change. This may be fun to tightrope walk on – but we would do well to remember that both chaos and order are still fictions made up by the mind in order to make sense of the world. Play with scale, and expand your horizons in space and time – whatever boundaries you choose, don't hold on too tightly.

Zen is an expression of a mentality which feels completely at home in this universe, and which sees man as an integral part of his environment. Human intelligence is not an imprisoned spirit from afar but an aspect of the whole intricately balanced organism of the natural world.
Alan Watts

Inside is outside.

In Permaculture Design there are countless reflective, engaging and instructive ways to survey the world that fit every personality type and every unique situation we find ourselves in – from looking for specifics like flows, patterns or edges, to noticing the boundaries, limits and resources in any given system. But the most potent way to survey, is observing from stillness, as it has the potential to encompass everything. Luckily, it is exceptionally straightforward to do, although that does not necessarily translate into it being easy – it demands a dedication that many of us are evidently not used to. However, when we might have time to sit peacefully somewhere with open eyes and gently receive the world, our attention may naturally end up following our breath and its soothing rhythm. Every day, countless times, the body asks for air to come and nourish it by creating a lower internal pressure in the chest with the diaphragm, which effortlessly calls the air to come rushing in of its own accord, filling up the lungs. The body opens the space and the air can't but help come. Then as we breathe out, seemingly relaxed and with minimum effort, we expel the old air back into the limitless space outside. The outside joins the inside, and the inside becomes the outside. This boundary between the two is also forever growing more abstract in modern science. We now know, for example, that there are vast colonies of microscopic insects living just on our eyelashes, and that there are more bacteria cells in our gut biome than human cells in the rest of our body. Where do I stop and the other begin? Where does interconnection become interpenetration? It is all one – we are the inside and the outside.

Engage in zazen as though saving your head from fire.
Dögen

How to sit (zazen).

Choose a comfortable place where you won't be disturbed.
If you can, set an unobtrusive alarm – this will stop you having
to check how long you've been sitting. Timelessness can be
a wonderful place. Sit in an upright position – a chair is
perfect – with your back and neck straight but not stiff,
your head gently sitting on top, and your hands in your
lap. Softly move from side to side, and sway back and
forth until you find your central balance. Stay in the present
moment by leaving aside all thoughts about the past and
future. As you become aware of your breathing, start to
focus on the physical sensations of your breath moving in
and out of your body. Notice your belly rise and fall, and
the breath entering your nostrils. Stay attentive to how
each breath is always subtly different. Very soon, you'll
wander off into some thought or other. This is normal, just
bring yourself back and watch these thoughts come and
go – whether they be pleasant or unpleasant thoughts, it

really doesn't matter. Don't try to change anything, as this is just what is going on for you in the present moment. This is what it's like to be you right now. Don't suppress or ignore any of the thoughts but treat them as if they are a radio faintly on in the background, always simply coming back to the in and out of your breath. Once your time is complete, quietly sit for a little while longer, allowing for integration of what just occurred, and giving yourself some space to come back to the rest of your day.

Awareness is observation without choice, condemnation, or justification. Awareness is silent observation from which there arises understanding without the experiencer and the experienced. In this awareness, which is passive, the problem or the cause is given an opportunity to unfold itself and so give its full significance.

Krishnamurti

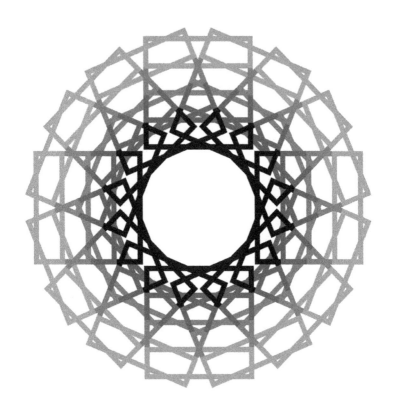

Chapter Three:
The web of connections

In which we integrate the use of Systems Thinking as Analysis...

These are powerful times, in which the world we have created has outstripped our capacity to understand it. We are experiencing a step change where complex human systems now operate within other complex systems.
International Futures Forum

Two monks were watching a flag flapping in the wind. One said to the other, "The flag is moving." The other replied, "The wind is moving." Huineng overheard this. He said, "Not the flag, not the wind; mind is moving."
Wumen Hui-k'ai

Zen is a special transmission outside the scriptures,
not based on words or letters, a direct pointing
to the heart of reality so that we might see
into our own nature and wake up.
Thich Nhat Hanh

More than the sum of its parts.

Systems Thinking is a useful, enlivening way in which to view this crazy world we find ourselves enmeshed in. And even if the whole is way too much for our small minds to fully grasp, it helps us have a reasonable guess at understanding where to jump onto the surfboard, and when to wait for the next wave. Originally stemming from the study of ecosystems, Systems Thinking is basically an academic way of learning from Nature. A system is any group of things or elements connected in such a way that they form a complex whole that has its own distinct behaviour. Viewed from this perspective, an animal, a transport network, or your current project can be considered a system – but not a heap of sand or something dead. Each and every system is a whole in its own right, and also part of a larger system. Think of single cells in organs in your body, or a person in a family in a community in a tribe in a nation – each element nested one inside another can also be considered a system in itself, depending where you chose to pay attention. Because Systems only have the borders WE construct around them. This is a radically different perspective from the old world, two dimensional, cause and effect understanding of life. Instead of being reductionist, boxing the world into separate bits, each of which tells only one part of the story, we can now look for synergy, where the whole is greater than the sum of the parts. A person is more than just lumps of muscle, bone and nerve tissue. What is this greater quality? What do we get from viewing something as part of a whole that we would miss from isolating it? Everything around us, including organisations, projects and communities, and even cities, cars and factories, are all part of and an expression of Nature – Systems Thinking looks at this all as a dynamic living process.

There's no need to carpet bomb, when a simple poke
in the eye will suffice.
Millie Baker

Nothing can exist on its own.

Systems Thinking enables us to be increasingly conscious
of ourselves and everything we're involved in, as
intrinsically and intimately interconnected with our
surroundings. Amongst the myriad of other things involved
in making this book, for example, were trees, foresters,
chainsaw manufacturers, drivers, car mechanics, paper
mills, publishers, computer industries, not forgetting all
the people that grew, transported and cooked their food,
and of course the sunlight needed to power the planet
at all. In fact, simply to be, this paper relies on the whole
order of things. How can we hold the wonder and
magnitude of this? Playing with scale and perspective
can help to understand how all the elements of a project
fit together like jigsaw pieces. It is useful to start from
a vantage point that can see as much of the puzzle as
possible – keep stepping back until it's all included in

your vision – even the bits you think you don't want. In fact, that which at first seems unwanted could prove to be the very piece that is needed – maybe hinting at an unrecognised shadow. This big picture overview will help you keep focus and hold you steady in the direction you want to go through your chosen landscape without getting distracted in the forest of fine print. Systems Thinking asks us to give our attention to the relationships between elements, as it's through these connections that we can learn so much, and therefore have influence and possible leverage to change outcomes – such as understanding how a chain of command operates, or mapping institutional allegiances in an economy. In reality, nothing can exist on its own, with everything impacting everything else in one way or another. Awareness of our own unique presence, as an intrinsic part of the world around us, can be deeply empowering, intellectually satisfying and liberating in unimaginable ways. No longer apart, we have come home.

Know the rules well, so you can break them effectively.
Dalai Lama XIV

Learn by playing.

Everyone can get a simple grasp of how to play the game
of draughts/checkers. Many of us, after some effort,
will figure it out and may even become quite fluent at
playing – maybe moving on to more complex board
games with seemingly infinite variations such as Chess
or the Japanese game of Go. When we learn the rules
of a game, we discover how each of the pieces move,
and identify the overall goal. Yet it is only when we start
to play that we slowly see how the game actually works.
We begin to notice that the pieces never work individually.
It is the relationship between all the pieces, yours and
your opponents, and the way they relate to the final
goal, which holds the key to understanding how the
game is played. So it is with using Systems Thinking to
look at the world. As the rules of a game dictate how
you play, so too do the rules of any system direct how the
relationships between elements will function and play out.

In government, this is expressed through laws providing incentives and administering punishments. The rules define a system's scope, boundaries, possibilities and degrees of freedom. Sometimes it's difficult to see all the constraints around you because they are so familiar – for example, many cultural rules and taboos may not necessarily be talked about, but if you broke them you'd know soon enough – try eating a pet or befriending a scapegoat. Permaculture demands that we hold its three Ethics close, so they inform our choices at every step; that way we have a compass when looking into the heart of each rule to glean its wisdom, even if that means going against the customs and laws of the society we find ourselves in. When we spend a few moments thinking about some of the rules we live our lives by and what behaviours they might engender, we quickly see their real power, and their potential to direct what is designed in our projects. How do you already play with rules in your life?

All is impermanent. Everything is in a state of
perpetual change.
Thich Nhat Hanh

Go with the flow.

Change being the only constant, we would do well to
embrace it and work with this inevitable fact of life.
In fact, life is energy in motion, forever changing
– each organism or organisation needs a continual flow
of energy to stay alive, be that food, sunlight, money or
labour. Life is never static, it's always either developing or
waiting, like a seed, as dynamic potential for a catalyst
to burst into development. It is said we take snap shots
of the world with our mind – as if our brains can only
handle small static chunks, not the real, more fluid
nature of reality. When we see things as frozen frames
or objects rather than as processes, we lose sight of the
fact that the world is in flux, always moving, even if ever
so slightly. Just as we personally are always in a process
of changing thoughts, emotions and body, so too do
mountains rise then slowly erode and offer their nutrients

up to the lowlands; multinationals grow from supplying to demand then break up or collapse; and innovative ideas become fashionable, then mainstream and finally obsolete. If, as Permaculture designers, we imbed this fact of constant change into our thinking, not only will our designs become more resilient but they will also become future-orientated, leading us to build in or nudge toward succession – a term used to describe the natural sequence of change that will happen in a system over time. If we have an idea of where a system is headed, we can also accelerate or slow down this Succession, taking advantage of any opportunities that pop up. A classic mistake, for example, is to plant a small one year old tree without having worked out how much shade it might cast once its canopy is mature, or starting a business but not actually having the right temperament to stay with it and make it a success. Curiously, change doesn't always manifest as we imagine – the world is a wild and complex place; who knows what could happen. Prepare to be surprised. Welcome change – as there is often nothing else to do but hang on to your hat, bear witness to what unfolds and be adaptable enough to work out how to put the new emerging puzzle together so it makes some sense.

A fallen flower

Returning to the branch?

It was a butterfly.

Moritake

Since my house burned down, I now have a better view
of the rising moon.
Mizuta Masahide

Dare to think abundantly.

Permaculture thinking is based on a radical
understanding and feeling of abundance, secure in the
fact there is enough for everyone's needs on this bountiful
planet. This is in stark contrast to the prevailing, insidious
feeling of scarcity in our current destructoculture,
which makes us all live in fear that there will never be
enough – so we end up hoarding – judging and valuing
ourselves and others by how much we have or consume.
Being able to witness life as it is, moment by moment,
rather than how we'd like it to be, uncovers its present
perfection. Living fully right now enables us to appreciate
what we already have, and one thing is community or
the possibility of community – so Abundance is trusting
in sharing. This sharing is how we already connect with
those close to us and how we build these connections
into community. This is making the most of any situation,

rather than constantly striving for an imagined and impossible perfection that always remains just out of reach. It doesn't mean there is nothing to be done, that we should never have wants, or there won't be people in need that rightly want to do something about it, such as the one in nine undernourished people on this planet. Neither is Abundance about living in the hope of a free energy future, or continuing to blindly act as if our planet's resources are inexhaustible. What would it be like to extend our capacity to share with those further and further outside our current sphere? Leaning into our personal Edge of caring until the entire world were included in our community. How would our lives be different if we dropped the fear and let abundance seep into our very beings, saturating our thinking until our decisions are borne from this feeling of plenty?

You could say paradigms are harder to change than anything else about a system [...] But there is nothing physical, expensive, or slow in the process of paradigm change. It can happen to someone in an instant. Whole societies, though, resist harder than they resist anything else. So how do you change paradigms? You keep pointing at the anomalies and failures in the old paradigm. You keep speaking and acting, loudly and with assurance, from the new one. You insert people into places of public visibility and power. You don't waste your time on reactionaries; rather you work with active change agents and with the vast middle ground of people who are open-minded.
Donella Meadows

The power of storytelling.

Permaculture, a portmanteau of the words permanent and culture (née agriculture), seeks to make conscious the particular paradigms that underpin our current society – and with this awareness set us free to choose the way we and our communities evolve. These paradigms manifest themselves in the shape of stories and beliefs that are passed from person to person, and have got us thus far. Becoming aware of our stories and how they affect our world helps us see which ones are no longer fit for purpose. Many damaging memes have riddled our culture like a cancer and driven us to this precipitous point in history that we all know so well, of dire resource depletion, terrible economic inequality, and insane biodiversity destruction. The very foundations of our civilization, the great assumptions of our current society – such as 'Growth is good', 'Nature is separate and needs to be tamed', 'Evolution stopped with Homo Sapiens', among many often very subtle and insidious others, must be reviewed, and if necessary debunked, denounced and composted. Stories that are regenerative and promote health of the whole system, our wider community, need to be savoured, nurtured and shared. So which of the current stories do you think we should keep, and which discard – and in the gap that opens up, which new stories do we so desperately need to design a thriving, healthy culture that won't inherently self-destruct?

Keeping oneself unattached in the arena of paradigms is to stay flexible, to realise that NO paradigm is 'true' and the universe is far beyond human comprehension. It is to understand at a gut level that there are paradigms, and to see that that itself is a paradigm, and to regard that whole realisation as devastatingly funny. It is to let go into not-knowing. There is no certainty in any worldview, and anyone that has managed to entertain this idea at all, has found it to be the basis of radical empowerment. If no paradigm is right you can choose whatever one will help to achieve your purpose. If you have no idea where to get a purpose, you can listen to the universe.

Donella Meadows

Chapter Four: The sharp sword of the Permaculture designer

In which we learn to design with attitudes...

We can design ways to transform our problems into spirals of growth, regeneration and well-being in all aspects of our lives.
Looby Macnamara

Every master who practices an art moulded by Zen is like a flash of lightning from the cloud of all-encompassing Truth.
Takuan

A designer is an emerging synthesis of artist, inventor, mechanic, objective economist and evolutionary strategist.
R. Buckminster Fuller

Right action.

The Permaculture designer is a rare breed – an honourable adventurer, a noble explorer scaling the cliffs of possibility whilst also unafraid to traverse the marshes of mundanity. They are consciously in service to themselves, their community and the planet – forever on the lookout for new, ingenious maps and models, hidden patterns, innovative, appropriate technology, deeply buried causes and subtly transforming effects. A hero's journey, but one more concerned with integration and grounded day to day living rather than grand gestures or peak moments. It is important you embark gradually – with yourself and your home, then purposefully extend outwards as your small circle of influence reaches further and further to meet your wider circle of concerns – your efforts rippling out into the world. Permaculture Design demands purpose and rigour, is based on system science, and is not for the wishy washy. If you want deep green earth magic, go find a shaman. If you want someone else to solve all your problems without having to make your own essential lifestyle changes, look for the latest fashionable greenwash – duping people into believing that we can leave the fate of the planet and its inhabitants to someone else. There is no messing – for it to be Permaculture Design, one needs to be crystal clear, not obscurely obtuse, thought through, not slapdash, sharp as a razor and wielded like a samurai sword, cleanly cutting through all the bullshit, clearing the smoke and sleep out of our eyes.

Primum non nocere (first, do no harm).
Anon

First do Nothing.

The very first thing to do as designers is Nothing.
Nothing at all. It can be difficult to not rush in and
involve ourselves, combat, conquer and generally
interfere, but Nothing is most likely the best option for
all concerned. Had many governments around the world
not bought into growing and using biofuels as a short
term antidote to climate change, there wouldn't be the
massive loss of agriculture land, deforestation, water
shortages, food price rises and ironically increased
usage of fossil fuels that we see today. History is awash
with embarrassing catastrophes caused by un-thought-
through endeavours from well-meaning individuals – from
salted fields ruined by over irrigation to increased air
pollution from traffic calming measures. Can you think
of other situations that would be better off being left
alone? We can never know everything, but the more
we wait the more we can garner just that little bit extra

from a situation. Take time, but this is not a hammock moment, zoning out, botanical cocktail in hand – this Nothing is pregnant, full of potent potential. It's in the Nothing-space that our Survey can begin in earnest, letting us observe from inner stillness – it enables us to rein in all the familiar knee-jerk reactions, uncouples us from uncontemplated ideas, and lets us wedge a pause for reflection between our thoughts to see if our insights, intuition or projections are correct. It's this wedge that can offer a world of difference, and open up a panorama of possibilities. There's no reason why you can't adopt a ponderous face for others while allowing the rest of you to catch up with your thoughts. As this active inaction is totally contrary to the current digital age of demanding immediate answers, you may sometimes have to wrestle impatient others, get them in a metaphorical headlock, a philosophical bear hug, or a logical full nelson, and simply wait a while.

You uncover what is when you get rid of what isn't.
R. Buckminster Fuller

Suspend agendas.

When designing, thoroughly examine your own sacred assumptions and opinions rigorously, and look carefully for disconfirming data. Ask your competitive peers, your experienced elders and especially your feared opponents and pedantic detractors. Invite others to challenge your ideas and add theirs to the mix. Instead of championing one theory, concept, process or idea, collect as many as possible – make it a hobby, collecting and swapping theories like football cards. Sort, grade and filter them – it's the only way to be sure any position is worth continuing with. Although you may know the direction you're heading, and may be clearly aiming for a final product or specific outcome, be watchful not to attach yourself to any previously imagined results. When you begin the Permaculture Design process, make friends with the scientific method by suspending all agendas, so you have no idea whatsoever what the end product will be.

This attitude can open you up to a world of possibilities. If any ideas do arise, park them in a notebook so you know they are captured for later reflection and no longer have a hold on you – drawing your attention away, like a catchy repetitive song. Your project may be to design your new home on a plot of land, and by staying open to the outcome you might end up working out that the best course of action is actually to conserve it as a nature reserve for the benefit of others. Or you may want to create a nature reserve and notice the real issue that needs to be dealt with is helping resolve a community conflict, knowing this must first be achieved before any meaningful other work can possibly begin. Make plans, create designs, but be prepared to abandon them when confronted with reality.

The plants and flowers

I raised about my hut

I now surrender

To the will

Of the wind.

Ryokan

When I am working on a problem, I never think about
beauty but when I have finished, if the solution
is not beautiful, I know it is wrong.
R. Buckminster Fuller

Dance designs into existence.

It is often difficult to accept things as they are – but
this is actually a radical way of changing the world.
Acceptance is not resignation, it is meeting reality.
So instead of pushing and pulling your ideas, forcing
square pegs into round holes with your will power –
dance them into existence. After all, it's often the subtlest
tweak that catalyses the profoundest change. Cultivate
a sense of play – juggle with all the elements in your
project. Take one perspective, then another, and then try
another again. Think outrageous thoughts, how daft can
you go? Try looking at whatever it is you're working on
through the lenses of the various Permaculture Design
Principles. Play removes tension, which frees our minds to
experiment a little longer than normal – curious to see
what unexpected solutions arise from the apparent chaos.

The trick is to go with the flow, design with rather than against Nature, gently waiting for insight or inspiration to arise, pushing you to leap, creating a domino effect. Simple cells in the body know where to align themselves, as do lifeless minerals on a river bed. When your mind isn't straining in concentration, something somehow perfect can pop up – some combination of relationships between elements that fit together in harmonious synergy. When designing a complex system it simply may take some time to let everything settle till it's just right. This can be frustrating, or it can be enriching – the choice is yours. With a patient, enquiring and calm mind, the answers become clear, things start to slot into place of their own accord and the design designs itself. You can tell a good design because it feels natural and beautiful. Look at Nature and the wondrous beauty around you – how it seems to effortlessly fit together – this is how we know whether something is working.

Die to everything of yesterday, so that your mind is always fresh, always young, innocent, full of vigour and passion.
Krishnamurti

Eternally curious.

Surely it is better to consider yourself a student designer rather than an accomplished one – a curious, mischievous learner rather a finished, polished product? The inquisitive, inquiring student will be ever vigilant of their weaknesses, will endeavour with single-minded effort, and have the space to improve – while the accomplished designer may think they know better, be lazy in their thinking, have a reputation to protect and bow under the pressure to perform consistently. If our design becomes a set of standardised actions – do this, then this, now that – or simply a collection of interesting techniques assembled together, then it is not Permaculture Design. Just as with Japanese calligraphy, where the experienced artist paints each character as if for the first time, Permaculture Design needs to be fresh, investigative questioning. However, it's not easy to see the world anew from moment to moment. It's not that this takes time to learn, just that such divergent thinking requires energy and insight — we can't seem to stop ourselves from using old well-worn formulas, favourite combinations of techniques or our own personal style. If you say "I used this technique the last time, I'll use another this time" you are making the same mistake — you are working from the old not from the new. The only way to be free from past ideas is to be vigilant, watch them arise, feel their familiarity and let them go. It may be that you settle with the same or a similar conclusion as last time, but no matter, this process will leave you richer and more assured of having chosen the right path. The question raised here is whether any decision made is an authentic, original action or simply a reaction?

You don't have a snail problem,
you have a duck deficiency.
Bill Mollison

Choose your attitude.

Positivity is the life-blood nourishing the body and mind
of the Permaculture Designer – it emboldens us to find
a solution where others just see a dead end, and to
fit all the pieces of a puzzle together into a complete,
congruent picture. If we look at the proverbial glass of
water half full or half empty, we know that in reality
it is ourselves that bestow any judgement on what we
perceive – one is not more true than the other. But, as
long as we're not beguiled into forgetting we're wearing
pink spectacles, or remain stuck as a Pollyanna, there is
no doubt that choosing to see the glass half full provokes
us to be far more visionary and inventive, and is clearly
a more enjoyable place from which to live in the world.
It is dwelling in this positive attitude that enables us to
see the potential of precious diamonds in dusty coal and
trusts that an elegant lotus can arise spotlessly clean from

a muddy bog. It is this attitude of boundless positivity that enables us to ingeniously transform issues previously seen as limits into resources. Seeing the problem as the solution has enabled Permaculturists to reframe the planet's possible coming energy descent, which many people find threatening and paralysing, as a potential platform for our society to design the world we want. The ability to choose our attitude has also proved very attractive to many despondent, battle-weary social and environmental activists who have burnt out, having spent all their strength and vitality railing against rather than building for. Knowing that a solution can be a seed within the problem at hand yields us a calmness and assured quality – this mental flip is a joyous creative act, and if you let it happen, it has the ability to open you to the limitless nature of the world.

If success or failure of this planet and of human beings depended on how I am and what I do...
HOW WOULD I BE? WHAT WOULD I DO?
R. Buckminster Fuller

This is it.

Permaculture Design is not about cleverly rearranging the deckchairs while your life and the planet's ecology slowly and painfully sinks into oblivion. It's not about ineffectual tinkering as the world breaks apart piece by piece, but a radical, unshakeable commitment to action. Permaculture Design is how we can actively and ethically express ourselves and our potential, how we act out our humanity – our sincerity and passion, our wonder and delight in this world. It's how we show ourselves and our commitment to our friends, family, and community, and how we manifest our lives in our environment. This is not preparation for something else. This is not the dress rehearsal. There is no time to faff and dither, to divide and argue. This is It. It doesn't get any more It than this. We need to wake up to conscious design, be vocal and take a lead to build a world we want to last.

If one really wishes to be master of an art, technical knowledge of it is not enough. One has to transcend technique so that the art becomes an 'artless art' growing out of the Unconscious.

D.T. Suzuki

Chapter Five:
Setting Sail

In which we are inspired into implementation...

When it is understood that one loses joy and happiness
in the attempt to possess them, the essence of natural
farming will be realized. The ultimate goal of farming is not
the growing of crops, but the cultivation and perfection of
human beings.
Masanobu Fukuoka

Flow with whatever may happen,
and let your mind be free:
Stay centered by accepting
whatever you are doing.
Zhuangzi

Your heart is full of fertile seeds, waiting to sprout.
Morihei Ueshiba

Step forward.

Sailing on the good ship Permaculture can be deeply
absorbing, highly enlightening and outrageously
exhilarating. Who knows where the winds and waves
will take you. You could find yourself reforesting denuded
areas of Belize, reversing desertification in the Sahel or
repairing overgrazed paddocks in Lincolnshire. Similarly,
you could end up healing broken communities in
Croatia, offering alternatives to prisoners in California,
or coaching social entrepreneurs in Hackney – or you
could just stay home; there is enough to do there too.
Once you've surveyed the landscape with keen
observation, analysed the info you've gathered with
Systems Thinking, and designed your plan till it hums with
beauty, you must commit yourself to implement your ideas
and leap into the unknown. Embedded in Permaculture is
this demand for action which understandably can often
feel overwhelmingly daunting. Our remit is wider than we

like to let on – none other than overhauling our entire relationship with each other and our environment – big stuff. There is much wisdom in the idea of thinking globally while acting locally, and when we speak of local we mean needing to garden our community as we garden our backyard – grow unlikely friendships, create guilds of mutually beneficial relationships, nurture exotic ideas, steer abundant energy flows and generally orientate life towards the health of the whole system, our planet and all its inhabitants. The world is your lobster, it's ready and waiting for you – what will you do? What tickles your fancy, floats your boat or makes you want to get stuck in? Every step you take ripples out waves of influence. Your inaction is felt just as strongly, and has just as many consequences as any action. So after a pause to gather yourself, why not step forward and find out?

Feel the fear and do it anyway.
Susan Jeffers

Dare to.

The whole landscape of possibilities has opened up in front of you, like the sun rising to herald a new day. But stepping forward can be challenging. You may be feeling unsure about your skills or quaking in the power of your own potential. It can be overwhelming to choose where to begin, but it can also be simple – start designing with yourself and your intimate relationships then work your way out from there to the environment where you live, your family, friends, colleagues, community, tribe, culture, bioregion, etc. When suddenly presented with something overwhelming or fearful, like being confronted by a tiger, humans usually deal with it in a number of ways. Fight or flight are two responses, but there are others, including the freeze response, whereby we become immobile, stuck, unable to make a decision, a sort of playing dead, which may include ignoring what is happening, apathy or even denial. There is also fawn, when we seek to flatter or suck up to our threat. Permaculture can offer a fifth way, 'facing' – turning towards, going with the flow, pausing with the moment and holding presence in what seems like a dangerous place, offering yourself up and surrendering to the possibility of being eaten by the tiger. Spaces that seem habitually fearful are often the places of greatest transformation – the juiciest sweet spot, the place of biggest leverage in a system, the Edge that only the bold and brave or innocent dare to consider. Surfing the tsunami is easy when you're a dolphin. Why seek out extreme sports, when everyday life experiences can be like leaning right over the edge of a cliff, dangling face down, but supported by a firm trust in yourself and your community. Prepare to feel your heartbeat racing, your nerves tighten, and then to translate what you call fear into the excitement of being on a real-life rollercoaster. Dare we? I dare you.

The temple bell stops,
But the sound keeps coming
Out of the flowers.
Basho

Pronoia: the feeling that unseen people are conspiring to help you.

Fraser Clark

Rouse a rabble.

It's probably an ancient inherited pattern, but we often expect someone else to deal with any mess we find ourselves in – a parental figure or saviour, an authority that will step out of the wings to sort out all the problems. Many myths, stories and legends confirm this in our day too, like the heroes from the movies, always saving the world. It is much easier to write history books focused on just one person, putting it all down to them, rather than the hundreds, thousands or millions of people that actually do the hard, day to day toil, often behind the scenes. However, we don't need to be someone with hero status in order to lead a project we feel passionate about – to do the work that we want, that is crying out for us to do. Putting on the shoes of leadership can also feel like the most comfortable, natural thing to do. Stepping into your own leadership doesn't mean having to put your ethics aside, in fact it serves everyone best when we act from a place of integrity and authenticity. With patient self-observation, find the block that stops you acting and use the fear around it as the energy to compel you forward into this new venture, use it as a trampoline jumping you into action – let everyone know what you're up to, put the word out and muster a team. Or you could simply look around and observe what's already out there, because someone else may be already engaged in something similar. The idea may have been growing for years just waiting for the type of person you are to join in before it can burst forth and bear fruit. Instead of reinventing the wheel, join them, band together to form a group, a community, a posse, a rabble, a force to be reckoned with. There are more and more people on this path together – there is a growing global community behind you, supporting you, wishing you well, egging you on. Simply intend to connect – keep yourself open to whatever comes your way and you'll find new friends and powerful allies popping up in the most unlikely places – especially in those places you think everyone is surely against you. Whether you step out alone or join forces with fellow pioneers, the critical mass starts here.

We are members of one great body, planted by nature...
We must consider that we were born for
the good of the whole.
Seneca (4 BC - AD 65)

Garden your community.

Humanity has all the information, ideas, concepts and strategies for our species to thrive on Earth, but this doesn't seem to be enough. For many years now, our world has had the technology and know-how to solve all the planet's problems – from widespread soil erosion and loss of biodiversity, to energy depletion and climate change. This convergence of crises is like a big stick sharply poking us in the ribs to wake up. Yet it is sometimes difficult to stay awake and acknowledge the situation we find ourselves in – and quite how far reaching the problems are, especially when many of us are simply keeping our heads down struggling to make ends meet. It's important to take this into consideration, as there is little doubt that it is ourselves who are generally the main limiting factor in any design. We need people, families, communities, bioregions, nations and cultures to catch up and get on board, and then spread the word further until ecological thinking, such as Permaculture, is the norm – embedded in the way we school, what we make and how we work. A fundamental shift in the way people see the world is essential if we're going to successfully make it through the next 10, 50, 1,000, 10,000 years and beyond. Part of our work in Permaculture is to continue to supply information to those that are hungry for it, but mainly to focus on people, and cultivate places for caring to grow, because goodwill can grow out abundantly in all directions, setting down resilient roots, spreading long branches and bearing bounteous fruit in unexpected places. The plants, the buildings, the mechanics are the easy part – growing a supportive, caring community and nurturing an authentic, lasting sense of place is much harder. So approach those around you where they're at, learn to speak their language, be patient, and lovingly tend to your community as you would your garden.

It is easy to believe we are each waves and
forget we are also the ocean.
Jon J. Muth

Offer your energy as love.

Relax into your journey – whether you choose a jaunty
step, a gentle amble or buoyant stride, enjoy yourself,
take in the scenery and remember the panoramic
perspective when pausing to savour the view. Along the
way there may often be a belief that in order to move
forward we need something else. This common dead-end
pattern keeps us stuck in fantasy, and will inevitably hold
us back from doing what we yearn to do because there
are always so many things that could be better – more
money, more skills, more knowledge, more help – the list
is endless. The stars don't need to be in precise alignment
for you to set out on your voyage, as Permaculture works
exactly with what you've got, with exactly where you're
at – so the time to start is always now. So open your sail
and let the wind propel you – work with Nature rather
than against it. This means acting with the capacity you

have. Who knows what qualities, skills and wit you're capable of – for you'll certainly surprise yourself. You are your own greatest asset – whose most valuable quality is your capacity for love. For the love that you pour into your actions will be felt by all those around for years to come. This Loving Kindness is the fertile soil that allows the germination of ideas to blossom into paradigm shifts, transforming your relationships with everyone and everything around you. By being who you are, by opening your heart, you will help others feel safe, encouraging them to do the same. This supports us all to connect more with Nature and the Nature in people, and in this place we naturally search for what is good for the whole and give that our full support.

When you touch one thing with deep awareness,
you touch everything.
Lao Tzu

Welcome home.

Your Permaculture journey will hopefully take you closer
home, where you've actually always been – closer to
yourself, closer to your community, closer to the Earth.
It is this closeness that will reward you with humble yet
powerful wisdom – the wisdom of intuition and insight
to know where to apply the subtlest of tweaks that could
make a world of difference, or when to wait just a little
bit longer. This intimacy yields empowering feelings of
belonging, trust and love that will enable you to be a
conduit for local and global solutions. Permaculture is
just one of many names for these solutions, part of this
emerging narrative, a culture of healthy abundance,
giving us the space and licence to co-create a beautiful
vision for the future.

We are part of a movement that is greater and deeper and broader than we ourselves know, or can know. It flies under the radar of the media. It is nonviolent, it is grassroots. It has no central ideology. A male vertebrate is not in charge. This unnamed movement is the most diverse movement the world has ever seen. No one started this worldview. No one is in charge of it. There is no orthodoxy. It is global, classless, unquenchable and tireless. This shared understanding is arising spontaneously from different economic sectors, cultures, regions and cohorts. It is growing and spreading worldwide with no exception. It has many roots but primarily the origins are indigenous culture, the environment and social justice movements. Those three sectors are intertwining, morphing, enlarging. This is no longer or simply about resources, or infractions or injustice. This is fundamentally a civil rights movement, a human rights movement, this is a democracy movement. It is the coming world.

Paul Hawkins

About the author

Intermittent beekeeper, occasional artist and erstwhile Shiatsu practitioner, Stefan is also an irreverent Permaculture teacher, avid mycophile and born-again hotelier (stathanshotel.com). He co-founded the London Permaculture Festival and the London Permaculture Network in 2010, and was Chair of the Permaculture Association, the UK's leading Permaculture charity, for five years. He also hosts the '21st Century Permaculture' radio show (21stCenturyPermaculture.com), and after dragging his heels for many years, is finally studying for a diploma in Applied Permaculture design. He lives and plots in north London. To see what's afoot go to stefangeyer.co.uk

Appendix

Recommended Permaculture Design books:

Permaculture Design
Aranya

Earthcare Manual
Patrick Whitefield

Permaculture: Principles and Pathways Beyond Sustainability
David Holmgren

Recommended Zen books:

Zen In The Art Of Archery
Eugen Herrigel

Zen Flesh, Zen Bones
Paul Reps

The Way Of Zen
Alan Watts

Hierarchy of resource use (from best to worst)

If you're going to use resources, have a method to your madness by always trying to find the best possible, or least harmful, solution at hand.

1. Resources that increase by use: e.g. coppiced trees, grass, some types of information.

2. Resources that temporarily disappear or degrade if not used: e.g. annual harvests, water run-off, some types of information.

3. Resources that are unaffected by use: e.g. climate, nice view, some types of information.

4. Resources that are reduced in the long term by use, e.g: mature forests, fossil fuels, jokes.

5. Resources that pollute or destroy other resources if used: e.g. residual poisons, radioactives, areas of concrete, gossip.

Permaculture
ASSOCIATION

Join the Permaculture Association

We are the networking charity in the UK bringing permaculture teachers, learners, practitioners and dabblers together.

Benefits of membership include:

● Learning   ● Networking   ● Events

Individual membership £24 a year
Group and Business options available.

Join today!   **t** 0845 458 1805

e membership@permaculture.org.uk

w www.permaculture.org.uk/join

Books to empower your head, heart and hands

For our full range of titles, to purchase books
and to sign up to our eNewsletter see:

www.permanentpublications.co.uk

Also available in North America from:
www.chelseagreen.com/permanentpublications

Before enlightenment; chop wood, carry water.

After enlightenment; chop wood, carry water.

Anon